July 15, 1992

Dear Sean —

To our very special Godchild
on his very special 4th birthday.

We love you,

Aunt Nita and Uncle Jack

D1303614

A CHILD'S BOOK OF PRAYERS

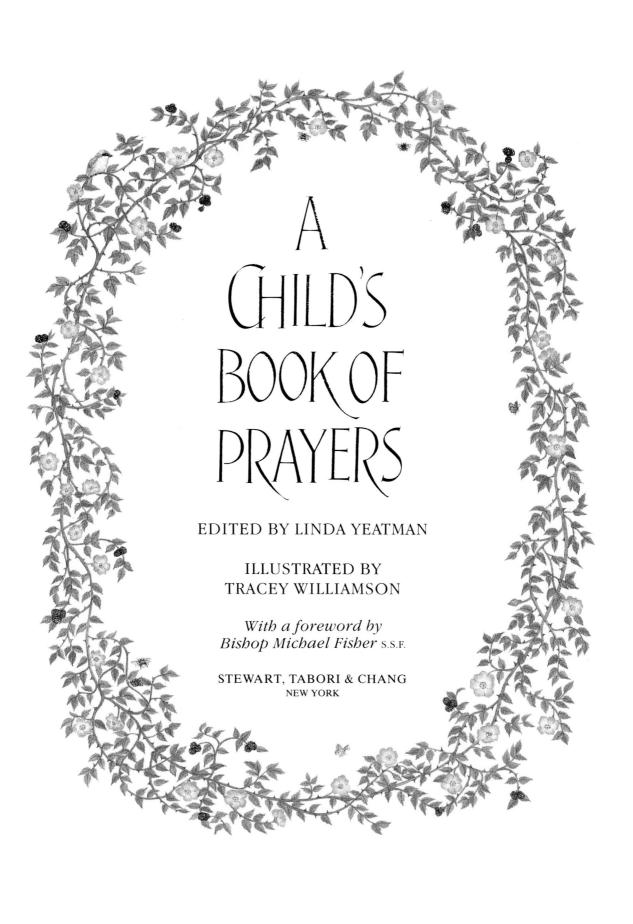

A CHILD'S BOOK OF PRAYERS

EDITED BY LINDA YEATMAN

ILLUSTRATED BY
TRACEY WILLIAMSON

With a foreword by
Bishop Michael Fisher S.S.F.

STEWART, TABORI & CHANG
NEW YORK

To Ianto
TW

Published in 1992 by Stewart, Tabori & Chang, Inc.
575 Broadway
New York, New York 10012

An Albion Book
Conceived, designed and produced by
The Albion Press Ltd
P.O. Box 52, Princes Risborough, England

Designer: Emma Bradford
Project manager: Elizabeth Wilkes
Permissions: Nick Wetton

Library of Congress Cataloging-in-Publication Data

A Child's book of prayers / compiled by Linda Yeatman : illustrated by
Tracey Williamson.
p.   cm.
Summary: A collection of prayers, grouped in such categories as
"Saying Thank You to God," "Asking God for Help," and "When God Talks to Me."
ISBN 1–55670–251–5
1. Children–Prayer-books and devotions–English. [1. Prayers.]
I. Williamson, Tracey, ill.
BV265, C473 1992
242'.82–dc20
91–37706
CIP
AC

Distributed in the U.S. by Workman Publishing
708 Broadway, New York, New York, 10003

Distributed in Canada by Canadian Manda Group
P.O. Box 920, Station U, Toronto, Ontario M8Z 5P9

Distributed in all other territories by
Little, Brown and Company, International Division,
34 Beacon Street, Boston, Massachusetts 02108

Typesetting and color origination by York House Ltd, London
Printed and bound in Hong Kong by South China Printing Co.

10   9   8   7   6   5   4   3   2   1

First edition

Contents

Telling God I'm Glad, Telling God I'm Sorry

Prayers for People Who Love Me

Prayers for Sad Times

God Loves Me and I Love God

Glad to Know You, God

Saying Goodnight to God

No dates are given for living authors

Thoughts on Prayer

There is a prayer about St. Francis that begins "Almighty God, you are always glad to reveal yourself to the childlike and lowly of heart . . ." St. Francis really was child*like*, never child*ish*, and prayers for children should be like that as well. We hope this book will speak to children of all ages; the sort of book that a child can grow up with and treasure through every age of life.

Whether we are young or old, God never talks down to us. God doesn't go in for "baby talk" and neither should we when we are talking to God.

The children in your life – other people's children as well as your own – will be helped most if they know you are saying the prayers *with* them, and not just to them or for them. Some of the prayers here will have words, phrases, and ideas that will be difficult for the youngest children, and will give you a wonderful opportunity to explain and help them to grow in their understanding of prayer itself.

Children develop "favorite" prayers; they are also good at learning quickly by heart, and this can begin before they can read. It is much to be encouraged.

Some prayers, phrases, and verses I learned as a child still flash into my mind – usually and comfortingly, in an emergency! It is a very good start in the life of prayer.

Use the prayers sparingly, and sometimes think about them or talk them over. Try not to rush it. If saying prayers is a part of going to sleep, that can be very good as well. This is a family affair between you and the children, and God, who is both Father and Mother as well as brother, sister, friend, and lover. Always, everywhere, at all times – and for everyone.

When children are faced with a very busy street to cross, a train rushing into a station, an extra big person, or anything a bit unexpected or possibly frightening, they instinctively find a hand to hold. They do it just as readily when they can't find the words to say "thank you" or "I love you." Praying is just as instinctive, holding out your hand to God. It is only later in life that we forget what children discover – the response, like a gentle and loving squeeze of God's hand. I pray this book will help to awaken prayer in children of all ages, and remind them of God's love for us, always.

Michael Fisher S.S.F.

Saying Good Morning to God

LORD JESUS CHRIST, BE WITH ME TODAY,
And help me in all I think, and do, and say.

Traditional

THIS IS THE DAY WHICH THE LORD HAS MADE;
let us rejoice and be glad in it.

Psalm 118: 24

MORNING PRAYER

Now another day is breaking,
Sleep was sweet and so is waking.
Dear Lord, I promised you last night
Never again to sulk or fight.
Such vows are easier to keep
When a child is sound asleep.
Today, O Lord, for your dear sake,
I'll try to keep them when I wake.

Ogden Nash

A Morning Song

Morning has broken
Like the first morning,
Blackbird has spoken
Like the first bird.
Praise for the singing!
Praise for the morning!
Praise for them, springing
From the First Word!

Sweet the rain's new fall
Sunlit from heaven,
Like the first dewfall
On the first grass.
Praise for the sweetness
Of the wet garden,
Sprung in completeness
Where his feet pass.

Mine is the sunlight!
Mine is the morning
Born of the one light
Eden saw play!
Praise with elation,
Praise every morning,
God's re-creation
Of the new day!

Eleanor Farjeon

LORD JESUS TAKE MY HAND
And lead me through this day;
Bless all I meet in home or street
While working or at play.

Lord Jesus take my hand
And let me never stray
Far from your side, but be my guide
In all I do or say.

Lord Jesus take my hand
And place it in your own;
Just hold me tight from morn till
night
And I'll not be alone.

Sister Mary Raphael

PIPPA'S SONG

The year's at the spring,
And day's at the morn;
Morning's at seven;
The hill-side's dew-pearled;
The lark's on the wing;
The snail's on the thorn;
God's in His heaven–
All's right with the world!

Robert Browning

DEAR LORD JESUS, we shall have this day only
once; before it is gone, help us to do all the
good we can, so that today is not a wasted day.

Stephen Grellet

BRIGHT MORNIN' STARS ARE RISIN'

Bright mornin' stars are risin',
Bright mornin' stars are risin',
  Day is a-breakin' in my soul.

Oh where are our dear fathers?
  Oh where are our dear mothers?
Oh where are sisters and brothers?
  Day is a-breakin' in my soul.

Some are down in the valley prayin',
  Some are deep in the mountain sleepin',
Some are up in heaven shoutin',
  Day is a-breakin' in my soul.

Traditional, Appalachia

Saying Thank You to God

WE PLOUGH THE FIELDS, AND SCATTER
  The good seed on the land,
But it is fed and watered
  By God's almighty hand:
He sends the snow in winter,
  The warmth to swell the grain,
The breezes and the sunshine,
  And soft refreshing rain:

> *All good gifts around us*
>   *Are sent from heaven above;*
> *Then thank the Lord, O thank the Lord,*
>   *For all his love.*

He only is the maker
  Of all things near and far,
He paints the wayside flower,
  He lights the evening star.
The winds and waves obey him,
  By him the birds are fed;
Much more to us, his children,
  He gives our daily bread: *Chorus*

We thank thee then, O Father,
　　For all things bright and good;
The seed-time and the harvest,
　　Our life, our health, our food.
No gifts have we to offer
　　For all thy love imparts,
But that which thou desirest,
　　Our humble, thankful hearts:

All good gifts around us
　　Are sent from heaven above;
Then thank the Lord, O thank the Lord,
　　For all his love.

Matthias Claudius
translated by Jane M. Campbell

FOR ROSY APPLES, JUICY PLUMS,
And yellow pears so sweet,
For hips and haws on bush and hedge,
And flowers at our feet,
For ears of corn all ripe and dry,
And coloured leaves on trees,
We thank you, heavenly Father God,
For such good gifts as these.

Anonymous

23

GIVING THANKS   GIVING THANKS

Giving thanks   giving thanks
for rain and rainbows
sun and sunsets
cats and catbirds
larks and larkspur

giving thanks   giving thanks
for cows and cowslips
eggs and eggplants
stars and starlings
dogs and dogwood

giving thanks   giving thanks
for watercress on river banks
for necks and elbows knees and shanks
for towers basins pools and tanks
for pumps and handles lifts and cranks

giving thanks   giving thanks
for ropes and coils and braids and hanks
for jobs and jokes and plots and pranks
for whistles bells and plinks and clanks
giving giving giving THANKS

Eve Merriam

PIED BEAUTY

Glory be to God for dappled things –
    For skies of couple-colour as a brinded cow;
        For rose-moles all in stipple upon trout that swim;
Fresh-firecoal chestnut-falls; finches' wings;
    Landscape plotted and pieced – fold, fallow, and plough;
        And all trades, their gear and tackle and trim.

All things counter, original, spare, strange;
    Whatever is fickle, freckled (who knows how?)
        With swift, slow; sweet, sour; adazzle, dim;
He fathers-forth whose beauty is past change:
        Praise him.

Gerard Manley Hopkins

FATHER, WE THANK THEE

For flowers that bloom about our feet,
   Father, we thank thee,
For tender grass so fresh and sweet,
   Father, we thank thee,
For the song of bird and hum of bee,
For all things fair we hear or see,
Father in heaven, we thank thee.

For blue of stream and blue of sky,
   Father, we thank thee,
For pleasant shade of branches high,
   Father, we thank thee,
For fragrant air and cooling breeze,
For beauty of the blooming trees,
Father in heaven, we thank thee.

For this new morning with its light,
   Father, we thank thee,
For rest and shelter of the night,
   Father, we thank thee,
For health and food, for love and friends,
For everything thy goodness sends,
Father in heaven, we thank thee.

Ralph Waldo Emerson

ALL THINGS BRIGHT AND BEAUTIFUL,
All creatures great and small,
All things wise and wonderful,
The Lord God made them all.

Each little flower that opens,
Each little flower that sings,
He made their glowing colours,
He made their tiny wings:

The purple-headed mountain,
The river running by,
The sunset and the morning,
That brightens up the sky:

The cold wind in the winter,
The pleasant summer sun,
The ripe fruits in the garden,
He made them every one:

The tall trees in the greenwood,
　　The meadows for our play,
The rushes by the water
　　To gather every day:

He gave us eyes to see them,
　　And lips that we might tell
How great is God Almighty,
　　Who has made all things well:

All things bright and beautiful,
　　All creatures great and small,
All things wise and wonderful,
　　The Lord God made them all.

Cecil Frances Alexander

FOR THE BEAUTY OF THE EARTH,
For the beauty of the skies,
For the love which from our birth
Over and around us lies.

For the beauty of each hour,
Of the day and of the night,
Hill and vale, and tree and flower,
Sun and moon, and stars of light.

Gracious God, to thee we raise
This our sacrifice of praise.

F.S. Pierpoint

GOD, WHO CREATED ME
   Nimble and light of limb,
In three elements free,
   To run, to ride, to swim;
Not when the sense is dim,
   But now from the heart of joy,
I would remember him:
   Take the thanks of a boy.

Henry Charles Beeching

30

LORD, I CAN RUN AND JUMP AND SHOUT AND SING!
I can skip and clap and stamp and SWING!
Thank you for making me alive!

Sister Frances Claire

LITTLE DROPS OF WATER,
   Little grains of sand
Make the mighty ocean
   And the beauteous land.

Little deeds of kindness,
   Little words of love,
Make our earth an Eden,
   Like the heavens above.

Little seeds of mercy
   Sown by youthful hands,
Grow to bless the nations
   Far in other lands.

Glory then for ever
   Be to God on high,
Beautiful and loving,
   To eternity.

Julia A. Carney and Percy Dearmer

Table Graces

FOR WHAT WE ARE ABOUT TO RECEIVE
May the Lord make us truly thankful.

Traditional

THANK YOU FOR THE WORLD SO SWEET,
Thank you for the food we eat.
Thank you for the birds that sing.
Thank you, God, for everything!

E. Rutter Leatham

SOME HAE MEAT, AND CANNA EAT,
And some wad eat that want it,
But we hae meat and we can eat,
And sae the Lord be thankit.

Robert Burns

DEAR GOD,
AS WE THANK YOU
For everything we eat and drink,
We remember all the hungry people
     in the world.
Help them as they search for
     their "daily bread,"
And help us never to waste
     or be greedy.
For the sake of Jesus Christ,
  Our Lord and theirs.

Michael Fisher S.S.F.

DEAR GOD,
WE THANK YOU FOR THIS FOOD
And everything you give us.
     As we remember all the hungry
     people in the world
Help us to help them
     For Jesus' sake, AMEN

Michael Fisher S.S.F.

BLESS, O LORD, YOUR GIFTS TO OUR USE
and us to your service; for Christ's sake.

Book of Common Prayer, Episcopal Church

PRAYER BEFORE MEAL

O Lord God, heavenly Father, bless us and these the
gifts, which we shall accept from thy tender goodness.
Give us food and drink also for our souls unto life
eternal, and make us partakers of thy heavenly table
through Jesus Christ.

PRAYER AFTER MEAL

O Lord, we give praise and thanks for your sacred
food and drink, for your manifold great grace and
goodness; thou who livest and reignest, a true God
till eternity.

Amish prayers

TABLE RULES

In table prayer be serious
And fold your hands in love,
Always in reverence lifting up
Your heart to God above.

And when the prayer is ended
Turn left and right expressing
To neighbors each your wish that God
Upon this meal grant blessing.

When the meal comes to an end
Be thankful for the food.
Be ready with great happiness
To pray in gratitude.

For God has called each one of us
His loving child to be,
That we may in our faith persist
To serve him joyfully.

from a Hutterite song

translated by Elizabeth Bender

35

When God Talks to Me

GOD BE IN MY HEAD,
And in my understanding;
God be in mine eyes,
And in my looking;
God be in my mouth,
And in my speaking;
God be in my heart,
And in my thinking;
God be at mine end,
And at my departing.

Old English prayer

O MAKE MY HEART SO STILL, SO STILL,
When I am deep in prayer,
That I might hear the white mist-wreaths
Losing themselves in air!

Utsonomiya San

PSALM 23 FOR BUSY PEOPLE

The Lord is my pace-setter, I shall not rush;
he makes me stop and rest for quiet intervals,
he provides me with images of stillness,
which restore my serenity.
He leads me in the way of efficiency,
through calmness of mind;
and his guidance is peace.
Even though I have a great many things to accomplish
each day.

I will not fret, for his presence is here.
His timelessness, his all-importance will keep me
in balance.
He prepares refreshment and renewal
in the midst of activity,
by anointing my mind with his oils of tranquility
my cup of joyous energy overflows.
Surely harmony and effectiveness shall be
the fruits of my hours
and I shall walk in the pace of my Lord,
and dwell in his house for ever.

Toki Miyashina

37

UPHILL

Does the road wind uphill all the way?
    Yes, to the very end.
Will the day's journey take the whole long day?
    From morn to night, my friend.

But is there for the night a resting-place?
    A roof for when the slow, dark hours begin.
May not the darkness hide it from my face?
    You cannot miss that inn.

Shall I meet other wayfarers at night?
    Those who have gone before.
Then must I knock, or call when just in sight?
    They will not keep you waiting at the door.

Shall I find comfort, travel-sore and weak?
    Of labour you shall find the sum.
Will there be beds for me and all who seek?
    Yea, beds for all who come.

Christina Rossetti

WHEN I PRAY I SPEAK TO GOD, when I listen God speaks to me. I am now in his presence. He is very near to me.

Anonymous

Out in the Fields with God

The little cares that fretted me,
    I lost them yesterday,
Among the fields above the sea,
    Among the winds at play,
Among the lowing of the herds,
    The rustling of the trees,
Among the singing of the birds,
    The humming of the bees.

The foolish fears of what might pass
    I cast them all away
Among the clover-scented grass
    Among the new-mown hay,
Among the hushing of the corn
    Where drowsy poppies nod,
Where ill thoughts die and good are born –
    Out in the fields with God.

Louise Imogen Guiney

OPEN OUR EYES
for your truth.

Open our eyes
for your will.

Open our hearts
for your love.

Open our hearts
for your joy.

Open our hands
for your work.

Open our hands
for one another.

Margareta Melin

OUR FATHER HEARS US WHEN WE PRAY.
A whisper can he hear.
He knows not only what we say
But what we wish and fear.

John Barton

LORD, TAKE MY LIPS and speak through them;
take my mind and think through it;
take my heart and set it on fire.

W.H.H. Aitken

Asking God for Help

A PRAYER FOR ASKING

Please give me what I ask, dear Lord,
If you'd be glad about it,
But if you think it's not for me,
Please help me do without it.

Traditional

TEACH ME, MY GOD AND KING,
In all things thee to see,
And what I do in anything,
To do it as for thee.

George Herbert

INTO YOUR LOVING CARE,
Into your keeping,
God who is everywhere,
Take us, we pray.

Traditional

LORD, MAKE ME AN INSTRUMENT OF YOUR PEACE.
Where there is hatred, let me sow love,
Where there is injury, pardon,
Where there is despair, hope,
Where there is darkness, light,
Where there is sadness, joy.

St. Francis of Assisi

JESUS, FRIEND OF LITTLE CHILDREN,
Be a friend to me
Take my hand and ever keep me
Close to thee.

Teach me how to grow in goodness,
Daily as I grow:
Thou hast been a child, and surely
Thou dost know.

Never leave me, nor forsake me;
Ever be my friend;
For I need thee, from life's dawning
To its end.

Walter J. Mathams

43

PROTECT ME, O LORD;
My boat is so small,
And your sea is so big.

Breton fisherman's prayer

GOD OUR FATHER,
   YOU HAVE GIVEN US A LOVELY WORLD.
Thank you for hills and valleys
   trees and flowers
      sunshine and rain
         animals and fish.
Thank you for my mother and father
   brothers and sisters
      relations and friends.
Help me not to damage your world
   but to treat it with care
      and to love all whom I meet.
Above all, teach me to love you, our Father,
   and Jesus Christ whom you have sent.

Donald Coggan

TEACH US, LORD
To serve you as you deserve,
To give and not to count the cost,
To fight and not to heed the wounds,
To toil and not to seek for rest,
To labour and not to ask for any reward
Save that of knowing that we do your will.

St. Ignatius Loyola

O THOU GREAT CHIEF,
light a candle in my heart,
that I may see what is therein,
and sweep the rubbish from thy dwelling place.

Prayer of an African schoolgirl

LORD TEACH A LITTLE CHILD TO PRAY
  And then accept my prayer,
Thou hearest all the words I say
  For thou art everywhere.

A little sparrow cannot fall
  Unnoticed, Lord, by thee,
And though I am so young and small
  Thou dost take care of me.

Teach me to do the thing that's right,
  And when I sin, forgive,
And make it still my chief delight
  To serve thee while I live.

Jane Taylor

47

O MOST MERCIFUL REDEEMER,
FRIEND, AND BROTHER
May we know thee more clearly,
Love thee more dearly
Follow thee more nearly,
For ever and ever.

St. Richard of Chichester

BE THOU A BRIGHT FLAME BEFORE ME,
Be thou a guiding star above me,
Be thou a smooth path below me,
Be thou a kindly shepherd behind me,
Today – tonight – and forever.

St. Columba of Iona

GENTLE JESUS, MEEK AND MILD,
Look upon a little child;
Pity my simplicity,
Suffer me to come to thee.

Charles Wesley

GOD GRANT ME THE SERENITY
to accept the things I cannot change,
the courage to change the things I can,
and the wisdom to know the difference.

Reinhold Niebuhr

Telling God I'm Glad,
Telling God I'm Sorry

LET ALL THE WORLD IN EVERY CORNER SING
   My God and King!
The heavens are not too high,
His praise may thither fly;
The earth is not too low,
His praises there may grow.
Let all the world in every corner sing
   My God and King!

George Herbert

GOD, THIS IS YOUR WORLD,
you made us, you love us;
teach us how to live in the world that you have made.

Hope Freeman

AT EASTER

Joyfully, this Easter day,
I kneel, a little child, to pray;
Jesus, who hath conquered death,
Teach me, with my every breath,
To praise and worship thee.

Sharon Banigan

GOD MADE THE SUN
   And God made the tree,
God made the mountains
   And God made me.

I thank you, O God,
   For the sun and the tree,
For making the mountains
   And for making me.

Leah Gale

Forgiving Others

Dear God,
I get angry when other people bully me,
   when they talk about me behind my back,
   and when they gang up against me.
Help me to forgive them.

I want to hit other people
   when they tell lies and shout at me,
   and when they say their parents are rich and clever.
Help me to forgive them.

Your son, Jesus Christ, shows us how to forgive;
He forgave those who crucified him.
Help me to stand up for myself without hating others.
Help me to be calm and strong when things get hard.
Help me to be more like Jesus every day.

I ask this in his name.

Alan Webster

FORGIVE ME, LORD, FOR THY DEAR SON
The ill that I this day have done.
That with the world, myself, and thee,
I, ere I sleep, at peace may be.

Bishop Thomas Ken

51

FORGIVE ME FOR THE ANGRY WORDS
    I didn't mean to say,
Forgive me for the fit of sulks,
    That spoiled a happy day.

Forgive me for the muddle
    That I left upon the floor,
The tea I wouldn't eat,
    The hasty way I slammed the door.

Forgive me for my selfishness
    And all my little sins,
And help me to be better
    When another day begins.

Kathleen Partridge

O GOD,
WE ASK YOU TO FORGIVE US
for
    the things we have not thought about
    the jobs we have not done
    the words we have not spoken.

We ask you to help us
    to think
    to do
    and say
the right things at the right time.

Brother Kenneth and Sister Geraldine

FATHER,
I WISH I HADN'T BEHAVED LIKE THAT TODAY.
I didn't really want to
But I couldn't stop myself.

There are two sides to me,
A good side and a bad side, and today
the bad was on top.

Please forgive me
I am truly sorry.
Help me to see my faults and to overcome them.

Help me, too, not to lash back when others hurt me.
Teach me to forgive them
and to treat them as friends.

Brother Kenneth and Sister Geraldine

Prayers for People Who Love Me

LOVE THE INWARD, NEW CREATION,
Love the glory that it brings;
Love to lay a good foundation,
In the line of outward things.
Love a life of true devotion,
Love your lead in outward care;
Love to see all hands in motion;
Love to take your equal share.

Love to love what is beloved,
Love to hate what is abhorr'd;
Love all earnest souls that covet
Lovely love and its reward.
Love repays the lovely lover,
And in lovely ranks above,
Lovely love shall live forever,
Loving lovely loved love.

Shaker hymn

GOD BLESS ALL THOSE THAT I LOVE
God bless all those that love me.
God bless all those that love
those that I love, and all those
that love those who love me.

New England Sampler

DEAR FATHER-AND-MOTHER GOD,
Thank you for my mother and father
and for all their love to me.
My mum is so loving and my dad so strong
I feel safe with them.
I want all children in the world
to have a happy home like mine.
It makes me sad to know
that many do not have enough to eat
and don't have kind doctors and nurses
to make them well when they are ill.
Thank you for sending Jesus
to tell us about your loving care
for your big family.
Dear God
I love you very much.

George Appleton

55

DEAR FATHER GOD,
You are so big, and I am so small,
Yet my hand fits so easily
Into yours,
And then I feel safe.
Thank you for all the people
Who hold my hand,
Even people who don't know me,
And especially when I am frightened,
And not quite sure you are there.
Dear Father God,
Thank you very much.

Michael Fisher S.S.F.

TINY TIM'S PRAYER

God bless us every one!

Charles Dickens

DEAR FATHER,
THANK YOU FOR ALL THE PEOPLE
who smile, and laugh
     and hug me – to show
     they love me:
And thank you for the people
     who really listen
     to show they love me:
And thank you for all the people
who talk and tell me real things –
     to show they love me;
And thank you most of all
     for the people, who in their
     own special way
     just – LOVE ME!
AND –
Please help me to love them,
in the same way. For Jesus sake, Amen.

Michael Fisher S.S.F.

MY FRIEND NEXT DOOR

Thank you for my friend next door,
And my friend across the street,
And please help me to be a friend
To everyone I meet.

Anonymous

LORD,

KEEP MY PARENTS IN YOUR LOVE.
Lord,
bless them and keep them.
Lord,
please let me have money and strength
and keep my parents for many more years
so that I can take care of them.

Prayer of a young Ghanaian Christian

MAY THE ROAD RISE TO MEET YOU,
May the wind be always at your back,
May the sun shine warm on your face,
The rain fall softly on your fields;
And until we meet again,
May God hold you in the palm of his hand.

Traditional, Irish

PEACE BE TO THIS HOUSE
And to all who dwell in it.
Peace be to them that enter
And to them that depart.

Traditional

A Child's Evening Prayer

Ere on my bed my limbs I lay,
God grant me grace my prayers to say:
O God! preserve my mother dear
In strength and health for many a year;
And, O! preserve my father too,
And may I pay him reverence due;
And may I my best thoughts employ
To be my parents' hope and joy;
And O! preserve my brothers both
From evil doings and from sloth,
And may we always love each other
Our friends, our father, and our mother:
And still, O Lord, to me impart
An innocent and grateful heart,
That after my great sleep I may
Awake to thy eternal day! Amen.

Samuel Taylor Coleridge

IN PEACE I WILL LIE DOWN AND SLEEP,
For you alone, Lord, make me dwell in safety.

Psalm 4: 8

60

Prayers for Sad Times

LORD JESUS, YOU KNOW THAT WE ARE SAD TODAY.
Help us to cheer up, because you love us always
and are close to us all the time.

Mary K. Batchelor

NEVERTHELESS, THOUGH I AM
SOMETIME AFRAID: yet put I my
trust in thee.

Psalm 56: 3

JESUS, WHEN I AM AFRAID, help me to remember that
you are with me, nearer than my breathing, closer
than my beating heart. You understand my fears better
than I do, so let me trust in you and give me the grace
to support others in their fears as you support me.

Janet Lynch Watson

LORD JESUS, I AM ILL.
Please make me well.
Help me to be brave,
and thankful to the people
looking after me.
Thank you for being here with me.

Zinnia Bryan

DEAR JESUS, YOU WERE TAKEN AS A BABY REFUGEE
into Egypt, take care of all homeless wanderers, of all
who have to leave their comfortable homes because
of misfortune or war, and of all who have no homes at
all. Guide them with your love to find help and
friends, and to help each other in their loneliness.

Janet Cookson

FEELING LONELY

I feel lonely today. Everyone else seems to have friends, but I don't. Help me to know that you, God, are a friend to everyone and that you are the best friend any of us could ever hope for.

Anonymous

HEAVENLY FATHER, BLESS THOSE WHO STARVE while we have plenty to eat; those who are homeless while we lie safely in bed; those who have no clothes while we throw clothes away. Help us to care for those less fortunate than ourselves and to do all we can to help them.

John Bryant and David Winter

DEAR LORD, IN YOUR WORD YOU TEACH US TO LOVE ONE ANOTHER. We ask you, dear Jesus, prevent war and bloodshed, prevent us and all the others from hunger and sickness. Let people stop killing each other. Forgive us our sins in your name alone.

Leonard H. Dengeinge,
12 years old, Namibia.

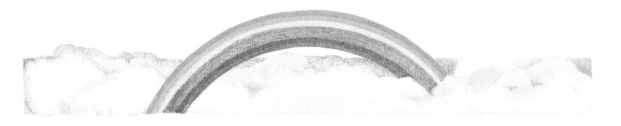

LORD JESUS, I PRAY FOR THOSE
WHO WILL BE UNHAPPY TODAY:
for mothers who have no food
to cook for their children;
for fathers who cannot earn
enough money for their families;
for children who are sick
or frightened;
and for those who are alone
and without people to love them.

Zinnia Bryan

DEAR LORD JESUS, OUR LITTLE DOG HAS DIED.
We cried because she was so loving and good. She
made everyone happy. We are glad it's you who've got
her now. Please take care of her, but of course you
will. You love all animals. You made them all.

Thank you for letting us have her first and for all
the happy times we've had with her.

Nina Hinchy

The Father of Us All

God our Father –
Jesus told me
I can talk to you.

I want you to tell my friend,
Who has gone to live with you,
That I love her still
And miss her so much.

You can help me
To be close to her
Even if I cannot see her
Because you are
The Father of us all

Michael Fisher s.s.f.

As the rain hides the stars, as the autumn mist hides the hills, as the clouds veil the blue of the sky, so the dark happenings of my lot hide the shining of thy face from me. Yet, if I may hold thy hand in the darkness, it is enough. Since I know that, though I may stumble in my going, thou dost not fall.

Traditional, Scottish Gaelic
translated by Alistair MacLean

LITANY

Gather up
In the arms of your pity
The sick, the depraved,
The desperate, the tired,
All the scum
Of our weary city
Gather up
In the arms of your pity.
Gather up
In the arms of your love –
Those who expect
No love from above.

Langston Hughes

God Loves Me and I Love God

AWAY IN A MANGER, no crib for a bed.
The little Lord Jesus laid down his sweet head;
The stars in the bright sky looked down where he lay,
The little Lord Jesus asleep on the hay.

The cattle are lowing, the baby awakes,
But little Lord Jesus, no crying he makes:
I love thee, Lord Jesus; look down from the sky,
And stay by my side until morning is nigh.

Be near me, Lord Jesus; I ask thee to stay
Close by me for ever, and love me, I pray;
Bless all the dear children in thy tender care,
And fit us for heaven to live with thee there.

Anonymous

Lord of the loving heart,
May mine be loving too.
Lord of the gentle hands,
May mine be gentle too.
Lord of the willing feet,
May mine be willing too.
So may I grow more like thee
In all I say and do.

Phyllis Garlick

What can I give him,
    poor as I am?
If I were a shepherd
    I would bring a lamb;
If I were a wise man
    I would do my part;
Yet what I can I give him –
    Give my heart.

Christina Rossetti

Two little eyes to look to God;
Two little ears to hear his word;
Two little feet to walk in his ways;
Two little lips to sing his praise;
Two little hands to do his will
And one little heart to love him still.

Traditional

DEAR FATHER,
   HEAR AND BLESS
Thy beasts
   and singing birds:
And guard
   with tenderness
Small things
   that have no words.

Anonymous

THEY BROUGHT YOUNG CHILDREN TO CHRIST, that he should touch them; and his disciples rebuked those that brought them. But when Jesus saw it, he was much displeased, and said unto them, Suffer the little children to come unto me, and forbid them not; for of such is the kingdom of God. Verily I say unto you, Whosoever shall not receive the kingdom of God as a little child, he shall not enter therein. And he took them up in his arms, put his hands upon them, and blessed them.

St. Mark 10: 13

LOVE GOD WITH ALL YOUR SOUL AND STRENGTH,
    With all your heart and mind.
And love your neighbour as yourself:
    Be faithful, just and kind.
Deal with another as you'd have
    Another deal with you.
What you're unwilling to receive,
    Be sure you never do.

Isaac Watts

Jesus said:

BLESSED ARE THE POOR IN SPIRIT: for theirs is the kingdom of heaven. Blessed are they that mourn: for they shall be comforted. Blessed are the meek: for they shall inherit the earth. Blessed are they which do hunger and thirst after righteousness: for they shall be filled. Blessed are the merciful: for they shall obtain mercy. Blessed are the pure in heart: for they shall see God. Blessed are the peace-makers: for they shall be called the children of God.

St. Matthew 5: 1

THE KING OF LOVE MY SHEPHERD IS,
Whose goodness faileth never;
I nothing lack if I am his
And he is mine for ever.

Henry Williams Baker

LORD, YOU KNOW THAT I LOVE YOU.

St. John 21: 16

Glad to Know You, God

O PRAISE GOD IN HIS HOLINESS: praise him in the firmament of his power.

Praise him in his noble acts: praise him according to his excellent greatness.

Praise him in the sound of the trumpet: praise him upon the lute and harp.

Praise him in the cymbals and dances: praise him upon the strings and pipe.

Praise him upon the well-tuned cymbals: praise him upon the loud cymbals.

Let every thing that hath breath: praise the Lord.

Psalm 150

SEVEN WHOLE DAYS, NOT ONE IN SEVEN,
I will praise thee;
In my heart, though not in heaven,
I can raise thee.

George Herbert

TAMBOURINES

Tambourines!
Tambourines!
Tambourines
To the glory of God!
Tambourines
To glory!

A gospel shout
And a gospel song:
Life is short
But God is long!

Tambourines!
Tambourines!
Tambourines
To glory!

Langston Hughes

THE CANTICLE OF BROTHER SUN

O most high, almighty, good Lord, God: to you belong
Praise, glory, honour and all blessing.

Praised be my Lord by all his creatures: and chiefly
by our brother the sun, who brings us the day
and brings us the light. Fair is he, and shines with
a very great splendour: O Lord, he points us to you.

Praised be my Lord by our sister the moon: and by
the stars which you have set clear and lovely in heaven.

Praised be my Lord by our brother the wind:
and by air and cloud, calms and all weather,
by which you uphold life in all creatures.

Praised be my Lord by our sister water: who is very
useful to us and humble and precious and clean.

Praised be my Lord by our brother fire, through whom
you give light in the darkness: and he is bright
and pleasant and very mighty and strong.

Praised be my Lord by our mother the earth,
who sustains us and keeps us: and brings forth fruits
of different kinds, flowers of many colours, and grass.

St. Francis of Assisi

HE PRAYETH BEST,
WHO LOVETH BEST
All things both
Great and small;
For the dear God
Who loveth us,
He made and loveth all.

Samuel Taylor Coleridge

HE IS KING OF KINGS,
He is Lord of lords.
Jesus Christ, the first and last,
No one works like him.

He built his throne up in the air,
No one works like him.
And called his saints from everywhere,
No one works like him.

from an African-American spiritual

LORD, THY GLORY FILLS THE HEAVEN,
Earth is with its fullness stored;
Unto thee be glory given,
Holy, holy, holy Lord.

Bishop R. Mant

GO TELL IT ON THE MOUNTAIN,
Over the hills and everywhere,
Go tell it on the mountain
That Jesus Christ is born.

from an African-American spiritual

WE CAN DO NO GREAT THINGS,
Only small things with great love.

Mother Teresa

GOD BLESS THE FIELD AND BLESS THE FURROW,
Stream and branch and rabbit burrow,
Hill and stone and flower and tree,
From Bristol town to Wetherby –
Bless the sun and bless the sleet,
Bless the lane and bless the street,
Bless the night and bless the day,
From Somerset and all the way
To the meadows of Cathay;
Bless the minnow, bless the whale,
Bless the rainbow and the hail,
Bless the nest and bless the leaf,
Bless the righteous and the thief,
Bless the wing and bless the fin,
Bless the air I travel in,
Bless the mill and bless the mouse,
Bless the miller's bricken house,
Bless the earth and bless the sea,
God bless you and God bless me.

Anonymous

O JESUS, I HAVE PROMISED
To serve thee to the end;
Be thou forever near me,
My Master and my Friend.
I shall not fear the battle
If thou art by my side.
Nor wander from the pathway
If thou will be my guide.

J.E. Bode

IN THE BEGINNING WAS GOD,
Today is God,
Tomorrow will be God.
Who can make an image of God?
He has no body.
He is the word which comes out of your mouth.
That word! It is no more,
It is past, and still it lives!
So is God.

A Pygmy hymn

NOW THANK WE ALL OUR GOD
    With heart and hands and voices,
Who wondrous things hath done,
    In whom his world rejoices;
Who from our mother's arms
    Hath blessed us on our way
With countless gifts of love,
    And still is ours today.

M. Rinkart

GOD IS AT THE ANVIL, beating out the sun;
   Where the molten metal spills,
   At his forge among the hills
He has hammered out the glory of a day that's done.

God is at the anvil, welding golden bars;
   In the scarlet-streaming flame
   He is fashioning a frame
For the shimmering silver beauty of the evening stars.

Lew Sarett

Saying Goodnight to God

LIGHTEN OUR DARKNESS, WE BESEECH THEE, O Lord; and by thy great mercy defend us from all perils and dangers of this night; for the love of thy only Son, our Saviour Jesus Christ.

Book of Common Prayer

GOD, THAT MADEST EARTH AND HEAVEN,
   Darkness and light:
Who the day for toil has given
   For rest the night:

May thine Angel-guards defend us,
   Slumber sweet thy mercy send us,
Holy dreams and hopes attend us,
   This livelong night.

Bishop Reginald Heber

NOW THE DAY IS OVER

Night is drawing nigh,
Shadows of the evening
    Steal across the sky.

Now the darkness gathers,
    Stars begin to peep,
Birds and beasts and flowers
    Soon will be asleep.

Jesus, give the weary
    Calm and sweet repose;
With thy tenderest blessing
    May our eyelids close.

Grant to little children
    Visions bright of thee;
Guard the sailors tossing
    On the deep blue sea.

When the morning wakens,
    Then may I arise,
Pure, and fresh, and sinless
    In thy holy eyes.

Sabine Baring-Gould

EVENING

In words of one syllable

The day is past, the sun is set,
    And the white stars are in the sky;
While the long grass with dew is wet,
    And through the air the bats now fly.

The lambs have now lain down to sleep,
    The birds have long since sought their nests;
The air is still; and dark, and deep
    On the hill side the old wood rests.

Yet of the dark I have no fear,
    But feel as safe as when 'tis light;
For I know God is with me there,
    And he will guard me through the night.

For God is by me when I pray,
    And when I close mine eyes in sleep,
I know that he will with me stay,
    And will all night watch by me keep.

For he who rules the stars and sea,
    Who makes the grass and trees to grow,
Will look on a poor child like me,
    When on my knees I to him bow.

He holds all things in his right hand,
    The rich, the poor, the great, the small;
When we sleep, or sit, or stand,
    Is with us, for he loves us all.

Thomas Miller

THE LAMB

Little Lamb who made thee?
Dost thou know who made thee?

Gave thee life and bid thee feed
By the stream and o'er the mead;
Gave thee clothing of delight,
Softest clothing woolly bright,
Gave thee such a tender voice,
Making all the vales rejoice:

Little Lamb who made thee?
Dost thou know who made thee?

Little Lamb I'll tell thee,
Little Lamb I'll tell thee:

He is called by thy name,
For he calls himself a Lamb:
He is meek and he is mild,
He became a little child:
I a child and thou a lamb,
We are called by his name.

Little Lamb God bless thee.
Little Lamb God bless thee.

William Blake

EVENING PRAYER

Watch, dear Lord,
with those who wake, or watch, or weep tonight,
and give your angels charge over those who sleep.
Tend your sick ones, O Lord Christ.
Rest your weary ones.
Bless your dying ones.
Soothe your suffering ones.
Pity your afflicted ones.
Shield your joyous ones.
And all for your love's sake,
Amen.

St. Augustine

GOODNIGHT! GOODNIGHT!
Far flies the light.
But still God's love
Shall shine above,
Making all bright.
Goodnight! Goodnight!

Victor Hugo

In the Evening

O Lord, support us all the day long, until the shadows lengthen, and the evening comes, and the busy world is hushed, and the fever of life is over, and our work is done. Then in your mercy, grant us a safe lodging, and a holy rest, and peace at the last.

Book of Common Prayer, Episcopal Church

The grace of our Lord Jesus Christ, and the love of God, and the fellowship of the Holy Ghost, be with us all evermore.

2 Corinthians 13: 14

The peace of God, which passeth all understanding, keep your hearts and minds in the knowledge and love of God, and of his Son Jesus Christ our Lord: And the blessing of God Almighty, the Father, the Son, and the Holy Ghost, be amongst you and remain with you always.

Book of Common Prayer

JESUS, TENDER SHEPHERD, HEAR ME,
Bless thy little lamb tonight.
Through the darkness be thou near me,
Keep me safe till morning light.

All this day thy hand hast led me,
And I thank thee for thy care.
Thou hast clothed me, warmed me, fed me,
Listen to my evening prayer.

Let my sins be all forgiven,
Bless the friends I love so well.
Take me home at last to heaven,
Happy there with thee to dwell.

Mary L. Duncan

O GOD, MAKE US CHILDREN OF QUIETNESS,
and heirs of peace.

St. Clement

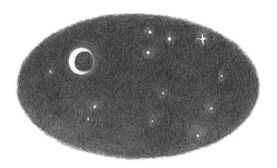

MATTHEW, MARK, LUKE, AND JOHN
Bless the bed that I lie on.
Before I lay me down to sleep
I give my soul to Christ to keep.
Four corners to my bed,
Four angels overspread:
One at the head, one at the feet,
And two to guard me while I sleep.
I go by sea, I go by land,
The Lord made me with his right hand,
If any danger come to me,
Sweet Jesus Christ, deliver me.
He is the branch and I'm the flower,
May God send me a happy hour.

Traditional

Now I LAY ME DOWN TO SLEEP,
I pray thee, Lord, thy child to keep:
Thy love be with me through the night
And wake me with the morning light.

Traditional

LORD, KEEP US SAFE THIS NIGHT,
Secure from all our fears.
May angels guard us while we sleep,
Till morning light appears.

Traditional

LORD, WITH YOUR PRAISE WE DROP OFF TO SLEEP.
Carry us through the night,
Make us fresh for the morning.
Hallelujah for the day!
And blessing for the night!

from a Ghanaian fisherman's prayer

THE LORD'S PRAYER

Our Father, who art in heaven,
hallowed be thy name.
Thy kingdom come.
Thy will be done on earth,
as it is in heaven.
Give us this day our daily bread.
And forgive us our trespasses,
as we forgive those
who trespass against us.
And lead us not into temptation,
but deliver us from evil:
For thine is the kingdom,
the power and the glory,
for ever and ever. *Amen*

St. Matthew 6: 9–13

Acknowledgments

The publishers would like to thank all the writers, publishers and literary representatives, who have given permission for quoted material. In some instances it has been difficult to track down copyright holders or provide a full bibliographic citation, and the publishers will be glad to make good any omissions in future editions.

African schoolgirl's prayer (No. 351): from THE OXFORD BOOK OF PRAYER, edited by George Appleton (Oxford University Press, 1985); W.H.H. Aitken: "Lord take my lips" (No. 244) from THE OXFORD BOOK OF PRAYER, edited by George Appleton (Oxford University Press, 1985); Anonymous: "Feeling lonely" from THE CHILDREN'S BOOK OF PRAYERS, edited by Louise Carpenter (Blackie & Son, 1988); Anonymous: "My Friend Next Door" from SIMPLE AND BEAUTIFUL PRAYERS FOR CHILDREN, edited by Arthur Wortman (Hallmark Cards, 1970); Anonymous: to the National Society (Church of England) for Promoting Religious Education for "When I pray I speak to God" from WORSHIP IN JUNIOR SCHOOLS; George Appleton: to Bishop Appleton for "Dear Father-and-Mother God" from THE CHILDREN'S BOOK OF PRAYERS, edited by Louise Carpenter (Blackie & Son, 1988); Authorized Version of the Bible: to the Crown's patentee, Cambridge University Press, for extracts from the KING JAMES BIBLE; Mary K. Batchelor: to Lion Publishing for "Lord Jesus, you know that we are sad today" from THE LION BOOK OF CHILDREN'S PRAYERS, compiled by Mary K. Batchelor; Book of Common Prayer of 1662: to the Crown's patentee, Cambridge University Press, for "Lighten our Darkness" and "The peace of God which passeth all understanding"; Zinnia Bryan: to Scripture Union Publishing for "Lord Jesus, I pray for those who will be unhappy today" from LET'S TALK TO GOD by Zinnia Bryan, copyright © Zinnia Bryan and "Lord Jesus, I am ill" from LET'S TALK TO GOD AGAIN by Zinnia Bryan, copyright © Zinnia Bryan; John Bryant and David Winter: to Hodder & Stoughton, Ltd., for "Heavenly father, bless those who starve" from WELL GOD, HERE WE ARE AGAIN (Hodder & Stoughton, Ltd., 1971); Church Hymnal Corporation: for "Bless O Lord, your gifts" and "O Lord, support us all the day long" from the BOOK OF COMMON PRAYER, (The Church Pension Fund); Sister Frances Claire: to the author and St Saviour's Priory for "Lord I can run and jump and shout and SING!" from THE CHILDREN'S BOOK OF PRAYERS, edited by Louise Carpenter (Blackie & Son, 1988); Donald Coggan: to the author for "God our Father" from THE CHILDREN'S BOOK OF PRAYERS, edited by Louise Carpenter (Blackie & Son, 1988); Janet Cookson; to Oxford University Press for "Dear Jesus you were taken as a baby refugee" from TIME AND AGAIN PRAYERS, compiled by Janet Cookson and Margaret Rogers (OUP, 1970); Leonard H. Dengeinge: to the Lutheran World Federation for "Dear Lord" from THE CHILDREN'S BOOK OF PRAYERS, edited by Louise Carpenter (Blackie & Son, 1988); Eleanor Farjeon: to David Higham Associates for "Morning Song" from THE CHILDREN'S BELLS (Oxford University Press); Michael Fisher S.S.F.: to the author for "Dear God, as we thank you", "Dear God, we thank you for this food", "Dear Father God", "Dear Father, thank you for all the people", and "The Father of Us All", copyright © 1992 Michael Fisher S.S.F.; Hope Freeman: "God, this is your world" from PRAYERS FOR CHILDREN AND YOUNG PEOPLE, compiled by Nancy Martin (Hodder & Stoughton, Ltd., 1975); Leah Gale: "God Made the Sun" from PRAYERS FOR CHILDREN – A LITTLE GOLDEN BOOK (Watson Publishing Co. Inc.); Phyllis Garlick: to the Church Missionary Society for

92

"Lord of the loving heart" from ALL OUR DAYS – PRAYERS FOR BOYS AND GIRLS, edited by Irene Taylor and Phyllis Garlick, first published by the Church Missionary Society, 1933; Ghanaian Christian: to the Church Missionary Society for "Lord, keep my parents in your love" (No. 140) from THE OXFORD BOOK OF PRAYER, edited by George Appleton (Oxford University Press, 1985; originally published in MORNING, NOON AND NIGHT (1976), edited by the Revd. John Carden); Ghanaian fisherman's prayer (No. 320): from THE OXFORD BOOK OF PRAYER, edited by George Appleton (Oxford University Press, 1985); Nina Hinchy: "Dear Lord Jesus, our little dog has died" from PRAYERS FOR CHILDREN AND YOUNG PEOPLE, compiled by Nancy Martin (Hodder & Stoughton, Ltd., 1975); John A. Hostetler: to the Johns Hopkins University Press for "Prayer before meal" and "Prayer after meal" from AMISH SOCIETY (1963); and "Table Rules" from HUTTERITE SOCIETY, translated by Elizabeth Bender (1974); Langston Hughes: to Alfred A. Knopf, Inc. for "Litany" from SELECTED POEMS, copyright © 1947 by Langston Hughes, and "Tambourines" from SELECTED POEMS, copyright © 1959 by Langston Hughes; Brother Kenneth and Sister Geraldine: to the National Society (Church of England) for Promoting Religious Education for "Father, I wish I hadn't behaved like that today" and "O God, we ask you to forgive us" from PRAYERS FOR CHILDREN AND YOUNG PEOPLE, compiled by Nancy Martin (Hodder & Stoughton, Ltd., 1975); Margareta Melin (trans.): to the Lutheran World Federation for "Open our eyes" from THE CHILDREN'S BOOK OF PRAYERS, edited by Louise Carpenter (Blackie & Son, 1988); Eve Merriam: to Marian Reiner for the author for "Giving Thanks   Giving Thanks" from FRESH PAINT, copyright © 1986 by Eve Merriam; Toki Miyashina: "Psalm 23 for Busy People" from THE LION BOOK OF FAMOUS PRAYERS, compiled by Veronica Zundel (Lion Publishing); Ogden Nash: to Curtis Brown Ltd. for "Morning Prayer" from THE NEW NUTCRACKER SUITE AND OTHER VERSES (Little, Brown & Co.), copyright © 1961, 1962 by Ogden Nash; Reinhold Niebuhr: to Ursula Niebuhr for "God grant me the serenity" from JUSTICE AND MERCY (Harper & Row Publishers, 1974); Kathleen Partridge: to H.E. Walter for "Forgive me for the angry words" from LITTLE PRAYERS FOR LITTLE PEOPLE; Pygmy hymn: to the Society for Promoting Christian Knowledge for "In the beginning was God" (No. 33) from THE OXFORD BOOK OF PRAYER, edited by George Appleton (Oxford University Press, 1985; originally published in PRAYERS OF AFRICAN RELIGION (1975), edited by Professor John Mbiti); Sister Mary Raphael: to the author for "Lord Jesus take my hand" from THE CHILDREN'S BOOK OF PRAYERS, edited by Louise Carpenter (Blackie & Son, 1988); Utsonomiya San: "O make my heart so still, so still" from THE LION BOOK OF CHILDREN'S PRAYERS, compiled by Mary K. Batchelor (Lion Publishing); Lew Sarett: to Lloyd Sarett Stockdale for "God is at the anvil" from THE COLLECTED POEMS OF LEW SARETT (Henry Holt, 1941); Janet Lynch Watson: to Hodder & Stoughton, Ltd., for "Jesus when I am afraid" from A PATCHWORK PRAYERBOOK by Janet Lynch Watson (Hodder & Stoughton, Ltd., 1976); Alan Webster: to the author for "Forgiving Others" from THE CHILDREN'S BOOK OF PRAYERS, edited by Louise Carpenter (Blackie & Son, 1988)